The Many Lives of Cathouse
Tales of a Rural Brothel

— bg Thurston

Červená Barva Press
Somerville, Massachusetts

Červená Barva Press
P.O. Box 53
Somerville, MA 02143

www.cervenabarvapress.com

Bookstore: www.thelostbookshelf.com

Photography: Tim Millunzi

Cover Design & Production: Tim Millunzi

ISBN: 978-1-950063-33-8

Library of Congress Control Number: 2025937605

*for Judith, Sarah, Hannah, Billie, and all the women
who have called this farm home*

&

*for my grandchildren: Sophie, Sam, Elias,
and Audrey Elle*

Acknowledgments:

Poems in this collection have appeared or are forthcoming in the following publications:

Family Celebrations, Andrews McMeel Publishing: "Epiphany"

Interface: "Night Frame," "Sky Meadow"

Jackson Homestead, Energy Necklace Project: "Procession"

New England Writers Anthology: "Whipple Farm"

Old Frog Pond/Plein Air-half a peck, 2014: "Heaven"

Old Frog Pond/Plein Air-Splash, 2016: "Darshan – Visions of the Divine"

Old Frog Pond/April, 2019 Poem of the Month: "Procession"

Quabbin Valley Voices: "Epiphany," "Sky Meadow"

Robert P. Collén Poetry Competition Finalist: "What Remains Sarah Weeks, 1856"

Smoky Quartz: "The Keeping Room," "Gratitude," "The Last Lady," "Richard Weeks' Lament, 1863"

The Copperfield Review: "The Lost Boy—Winfield Scott Weeks (1847-1856)"

The Longfellow Society Journal: "The Ruined House"

The Mud Chronicles: "Spring Forward," "Christmas Day"

The Muddy River Review: "Lineage," "Caleb Weeks, 1805." "Everlings," "Speakeasy, 1935," "The Ghost"

The Red Letter Poem Project: "Gratitude"

Worcester Public Library, StoryLine Poem Project: "Procession"

"Destination," "Whipple Farm," "Home Restoration," and "The Ruined House" appeared in Nightwalking ©2011, published by Haleys of Athol.

"Whipple Farm" also appeared in Saving the Lamb ©2007 published by Finishing Line Press, Georgetown, Kentucky.

***

The research for this book began in earnest on a winter afternoon in 2011 when I was summoned for jury duty at the Greenfield, Massachusetts Courthouse. While waiting to be dismissed, I wandered up to the floor that housed the Registry of Deeds. It was there I discovered the probate records for Caleb Weeks' estate as well as widow Sarah Weeks' 1856 petition asking the court to allow her to retain her few possessions from being sold at auction. From those documents, I continued with this journey to find as much verifiable information about the many inhabitants of our farmhouse as possible. During the decade of searching for any written or photographic information, I started to intuit what their lives must have been like. Many of them became so familiar to me that I began writing about them. My most important concern while working on this book has been to represent their lives with respect, honesty, and compassion.

I am deeply grateful to Gloria Mindock for her expert editorial guidance and willingness to publish this volume. It would not exist without her help. I am indebted to the three critique groups who gave me valuable suggestions for these poems. I am also thankful to dear friends who read this manuscript and offered generous feedback and advice: Candace Curran, Judith Ferrara, Clare Green, Sharon Harmon, Linda Hoffman, Elizabeth Lund, Susan Roney O'Brien, Susan Edwards Richmond, and Ruth Silin. Many thanks to my fellow Warwickians for their encouragement and many anecdotes about our colorful farm. Lastly, thank you Tim—you make everything possible.

Table of Contents:

If Light is in your Heart you will find your way Home
—Rumi

-I-

In the spring of 2000, I drove the backroads home from graduate school in Vermont. Following a narrow dirt road to the top of a small mountain, I crossed the New Hampshire state line bordering Massachusetts. Somewhere near the crest, I spotted a small red farmhouse nestled behind tall sugar maples. Two horses were grazing in the pasture. There was a "For Sale" sign in front. I jotted down the number in my notebook. My dream had always been to own and live on a farm.

Beginnings

In the north central region of Massachusetts, the land that became this remote small town was first known by its Indian name of "Shaomet." In 1744, the early English settlers renamed the town "Roxbury Canada."

The origins of Cathouse Farm go back to 1735, when the court for the Majestic's Province in Massachusetts Bay voted to grant four tracts of land, each six miles square in the western areas of the province. The tracts were divided into sixty-three equal shares of fifty acres, three of which were to be used for the minister, the meeting house, and a school. The sixty remaining lots were awarded to petitioners with preference given to the descendants of the soldiers and officers serving in the 1690 Canadian expedition. The 62nd lot is what became the location for this farm. The 61st lot located across the road became Whipple Farm, which is still owned by the descendants of the original family today.

When the town was incorporated on February 17, 1763, it was renamed once more and became "Warwick," in honor of the Earl of Warwick. Warwick remains a mostly rural town of about 780 residents and large tracts of forested state land.

Destination

You must go find the key
for your farmhouse.

Where is it?
  Hidden at the back
  of the black mailbox.

What should I take?
  Clean water in a cut glass jar
  and a sense of trespass.

What will I do there?
  Feast on the letters of the dead.

Will anyone know me?
  You will be known
  only by your house's name.

How do I get to this place?
  Find the collapsed barn
  where four roads meet.

Whom will I see?
  An old farmer holding
  a bloody head by its horn.

What should I ask him?
  Don't speak. Turn left at the corner,
  proceed until the dirt lane ends.

How will I know for sure?
  You won't.

3

Procession

I was holding down a convulsing ewe,
when my friend said *People need to know
that farming isn't a Norman Rockwell painting.*

No one understands why I want to live here
in the middle of nowhere, at the end of the line.
Sometimes I cannot remember myself.

My great-grandfather, Charles Bartholomew Lorenz,
was a dairy farmer in Waterford, Pennsylvania.
My other ancestors raised sheep and crops.

Farming comes with its own stark language:
ring-womb, wool-break, star-gazing, milk fever.
One learns to pay attention to nature's signs.

Life and death entwine here every single day
and all I am certain of is that I am not in control
of what survives and what will escape my grasp.

But each day, I pray and try to stay patient.
Sometimes I even remember the reason I am
rooted so deeply to this earth—to raise up

these living, breathing beings. The ewe recovers
and her twin lambs gambol around her.
Crocuses bloom in places I did not plant them,

silent hands stretching up from the soil, offering
comfort from kin I never met, a legacy of knowing
this is the only place I belong.

The Ghost

I have not left the world
It was poetry who abandoned me
                    Or so I believed
Now when I hold my hands over my ears
I see the echo from the sparrow's throat
And when I close my eyes tight
I smell the color of blood and rust
Holding my palm over my heart
                    I feel nothing
As words continue falling all around my feet.

Whipple Farm

Inside the abandoned house with its torn-off door, piles of galvanized nails and deer scat cover wide chestnut planks. I lift plastic film from the broken window of another century when a woman sweeps pine pollen out of the open doorway, her blue calico skirt rising with gold dust. She tucks a strand of dark hair behind each ear and hears a familiar mocking from the leafless catalpa. She places one hand over her stomach to feel the quickening. A slight breeze saves her from the sudden heat, scenting humid air with a heady blossoming of lilacs.

Bad luck to pick some for her babies' graves. Or to take a bouquet to her mother in the village where four townsfolk sickened last week with pox-fever. Along the lane the fox waves his plumy red tail, his coat glinting with sun, sleek from feeding on her best hens. All day her husband toils in the lower pasture, fitting flat stones into a wall that will outlast him. Brown-faced cattle chew and swat flies with matted tails. When he pauses to wipe the sweat from his neck, he imagines her waist thickening and begins to whistle.

Sister Houses, 1775

We were built from the same forest
and from afar, we look the same,
set across from each other on a dirt
road that snakes up the south side
of a mountain covered in fir and oak.

Our rooms smelled of woodsmoke,
kerosene, and endless cooking.
We shared families and children's
laughter as they ran up and down
staircases and around the hearth.

Pine-scrubbed tables bore dark rings
from coffee mugs and cups of tea,
where crumbs of conversation fell
into cracks in wide-plank floors, worn
smooth from heavy boots and sweeping.

Between us, sugar maples lined the land
cleared for cow pastures and orchards.
Everywhere, stone walls and stacks
of firewood grew, amid the earthen scent
of rain and mud and dung. Hard work

was the religion our people believed in.
Though the chapel bell in the valley
called them away each sabbath, sweat
washed from their faces and good clothes.
They sang hymns of here and Heaven.

Generations lived and left one by one.
Now deer bed down under apple trees
where we remain, faithful to the last,
silhouettes sleeping in a sepia landscape
bathed in moonlight, sheltered by sky.

Christmas Day

Onto the wooded path
my dogs pull me past
the thinking rock.
The air is still and cold,
bathed in that strange half-light
of almost dusk.
It has not been a year
where words were easy.
The ordinary miracles
piled up, unrecorded.
Here the pines sigh, hushed
by robes of snow as the dogs
glory in icy tracks
of creatures who have passed,
the only proof of those
we cannot see or hear.

Lineage

Seeking the genealogy of this house and land
is like piecing a spirit quilt together—
The same names repeat every generation:
Caleb, Sarah, Richard, Hannah, William, and Mary.
Their children appear and disappear suddenly—
Lung Fever, Croup, Bornstill, oftentimes
taking their mother with them into the grave.
Reading elegant script belies the somber tone
of each recorded event. Bewildered, I stand
under the evening sky and question what I have
in common with the women who have lived
on this acreage. I lift my head when I hear
them whisper in a sky bright with stars—
the unchanging patterns all of us share.

-II-

The older residents of Warwick told me stories about the house being built by Revolutionary War soldiers which made me curious. I began investigating the farm's origins and the people who lived here since the 1700's. Most of them were farmers who endured the challenges of keeping their families warm, safe, and fed.

The Weeks Family
1770-1870

In the 1770's, two brothers, William and Samuel Weeks took possession of their family's land grant and built a two-story cape post and beam house on the northwestern corner of the acreage. It appears that both William and Samuel enlisted as soldiers in the Revolutionary War before moving into the house. Their older brother, Richard, and his wife, Judith, were the first recorded Weeks family to live in the house on what is now Cathouse Farm. They had seven children including their son Caleb, who inherited the farm in 1813 and was married to Sarah. She gave birth to nine children.

Caleb and Sarah's son, Richard, took over the farm in 1855 after his father's passing, and was married to Hannah. Richard and Hannah lived during the period when deadly epidemics plagued the colonies, including smallpox, yellow fever, and cholera. Of their eight children, three sons died in childhood. This likely contributed to their decision to leave the family farm in 1863. Richard passed away soon after in 1868 and Hannah died of consumption the following year, leaving their daughters and their last son, Frederick Daniel, an orphan at five years old.

Judith Speaks, 1800

I am the bride who survived
the hardships of homesteading
to tame this wild, rocky land,

the matriarch of everything
that follows when my son, Caleb,
and his wife, Sarah, inherit.

I am the force that rocks a chair
in the corner of the keeping room,
making sure the children behave.

Now, I am a widow wearing black
aprons with deep hidden pockets
lined with horehound and tears.

I am the distaff of the flax wheel,
spinning out these long yarns
of family and furthermore.

Caleb Weeks, 1805

He pauses to lean against the door
and watch early evening descend,
takes a swig of cider from the flask
tucked behind the slatted feed bin.
A good day, another acre plowed
to plant potatoes and field corn.

Lifting the harness and traces
from the sorrel horse, he leads him
into the dark barn. One tin scoop
of oats, then several forkfuls of hay
pitched from high in the mow.
Swallows peer down from rafters.

He breathes the scent of timothy
mixed with sweat and manure.
For him, there is no better chapel
than these weathered wooden walls,
listening to the contented chorus
of chewing from the animals he loves.

To the Hon. Judge of Probate for the County of Franklin

The Subscriber widow of the late Caleb Weeks Asks your Hon. to give unto me the following articles of furniture which have been appraised, in Addition to my Lawful right in the estate

widow   Sarah Weeks
         Richard Weeks
         Hannah Fisher

To 1 Bed	6.00
1 Bureau or Case draws	2.00
1 Bible	1.00
1 Rocking Chair	1.50
1 Table	2.00
1 Chairs	1.25
1 Chest	.25
1 Lightstand	.50
	$14.50

What Remains - Sarah Weeks, 1856

I have labored long for all
these years on this forlorn farm,
birthed and buried our babies—
once within the same week.

Caleb was a husband as good
as he could manage. Summers
he chopped wood and plowed
furrows deeper into his brow.

I kept my part of our bargain
but in the end, have little to show.
And now Caleb lies in the same
ground that grew mostly stones.

Intestate: in the end he had no will.
Now I pray and plead with the Lord
and the court, petition a probate judge
to allow me to keep what was mine:

my bed, a bureau, my Bible,
and my rocking chair, one table,
a chest and a single lightstand.
The rest all gone, sold off to pay

the debt that grew each season
when the crops died or the cow
dried up. Caleb had his bottle
and I my psalms and prayers.

Alone, rocking, I remember
my Caleb pulling me close—
his ragged breath, his rough palms
burrowing under the worn quilt of night.

Hannah Speaks, 1860

Most of my forty-two years,
I worked this farm with Richard.
Summers spent chopping firewood
and growing enough to feed us all.

The few women who lived nearby
were comfort. We gathered scraps
of gossip stitched to the whisper
of needles and thread and pieces

of worn dresses and torn shirts.
Someone was always with child,
hands folded above the swelling
while the rest guessed girl or boy.

But mostly, I worked and cooked,
cleaned and washed all we had.
We grew corn and potatoes,
raised cattle, a sow, and sheep.

My flowers were always wild ones
but I loved the pale purple blossoms
of pole beans best and the brambles'
snowy blooms and thorns and berries.

When evening chores were finished,
with the sun sinking behind the pines
in the upper pasture, I'd close my eyes
and listen for the deer to come in quiet

and browse beneath the orchard trees,
where a mockingbird sat singing
all he heard that long, God-filled day—
my husband and children sound asleep.

The Lost Boy—
  Winfield Scott Weeks (1847-1856)

watches from the front window,
murmurs as he strokes the ears
of his smooth collie, who thumps
her long tail, hoping for a walk.

The rooms are empty, the hearth
cold and quiet, but he remembers
his mother singing as she stirred
the iron kettle and kneaded bread.

He had held his father's last hope
along with his mother's heart.
But when he died, his family
took their grief and moved away.

He never met his younger brother,
Frederick, orphaned at five years,
who grew to work in the wool trade
then started his own shoddy mill.

His sisters married, assumed other
names, and had their own children.
Now they lie next to husbands
in graves far from this old farm.

Across the road, the sky glows
red, then orange as the sun sets
past the hayfield where Jersey cows
line up at the milk barn gate.

He hears his mother's distant calls
but he is not ready to join her.
Some souls stay tethered to a place—
for him, this home is heaven enough.

18

Lottie's Dream
for Charlotte H. Weeks (1853 - 1875)

When muddy spring arrives, Mother
has me on my knees, planting beans,
while I slap at flies with filthy hands.

I memorize vocabulary words and recite
arithmetic sums inside my sweaty forehead:
j-o-u-r-n-e-y, *13X8 =104*, *f-o-r-l-o-r-n.*

When Mother returns inside to prepare
supper for Father and my three brothers,
I sneak away, past the smelly barnyard,

through stubby cornfields, then disappear.
I slip into the cool, darkening woods,
walk till I hear the swollen creek gushing

over rocks. The slush and spring-melt
from the mountain rushes down a narrow
channel that begins here on our farmland

then travels east. I dip my fingers clean
into icy, clear water, watch it tumble
wild and free from any responsibilities.

Papa says that these same drops flow
into streams, then rivers, then all the way
out to the harbor in the Atlantic Ocean.

Soon, I plan to leave and live in Boston
and if I get my way, attend the Teachers'
College where I'll discover everything,

and find out the secrets I will never learn
still stuck on this farm, dreamily weeding
dreary rows of boredom and endless beans.

Richard Weeks' Lament, 1863

In the year before last,
I still wanted to believe
our troubles would vanish,

but a stubborn evil persists
and plants itself inside
every crevice and crack

of this faltering landscape,
where planks from the fallen
barn litter the fallow fields.

All my heart tells me
is to take up my family
and leave this forlorn place,

the house where I was born,
our footsteps on the cart path
now erased by snow. Gone—

all the ways we were held here.
Our places around the long table
in the gathering room sit empty.

We do not know where we
will go. Our prayers will light
our way. God save our souls.

Barrus Cemetery
Richmond, New Hampshire

I kneel on the graves in this wild place,
plant violets and seeds of forget-me-nots
around headstones with faded names.

A stream nearby tumbles over rock
as ferns unfurl and birds chatter
from thickets of choke cherries.

Ravaged by hurricanes and neglect,
the markers lie skewed and broken.
Four generations are buried here:

Judith and Richard lie beneath
slate slabs next to Hannah,
their first daughter, nine years old.

Down the line, Sarah and Caleb
and their daughter Laura, one year,
by worn posts with carved initials.

Near the back wall of mossy granite,
lie Hannah and Richard with sons
Irving, Everett, and Winfield Scott.

Three small stones for three short lives,
cut by dropsy, croup, and cholera.
One orphan, Frederick, the only survivor.

I wonder how you survived the challenges
and sorrow of that primitive time, visited
by the pestilence that creepeth in darkness.

Two-hundred-and-fifty years later, I return
to the home you built, all of us sheltered
by a simple house of posts and beams.

-III-

Though most of the surrounding lands are forested conservation land owned either privately or by the State of Massachusetts, we were fortunate to purchase the five acres on the north boundary that once were part of the original land grant. Presently the farm has more than 33 acres of the original 50 and abuts the Massachusetts/New Hampshire line.

Turbulent Times
1876-1999

During the tumultuous times of the Civil War, World War I, and the Great Depression, the house changed ownership eleven times. It went into foreclosure twice and was put up at public auction once. Finally, during the era of Prohibition, the farm fell into the hands of George F. Rivers, who decided to set the property up as a speakeasy and rural brothel. He also purchased the farmhouse up the road, just across the state line in Richmond, New Hampshire.

When the Massachusetts agents would come to raid the premises, he simply moved his operation and the ladies to the New Hampshire house and vice versa when the New Hampshire authorities came to raid that property. Finally, the two states coordinated their efforts and conducted raids at the same time, resulting in George Rivers' arrest and incarceration. During his time in prison, he deeded the property over to his housekeeper, Bernice (Billie) Wysk. She again took ownership after Rivers' mortgage default in 1954 and continued to live on the farm until almost 1990.

Heyday, 1910
—from the Franklin County Registry
of Deeds, May 22, 1910

"Know all Men by these Presents that I, Alfred Swanson of Warwick in the County of Franklin and State of Massachusetts, for and in consideration of the sum of Twelve Hundred & Fifty Dollars to me in hand, for the delivery hereof, well and truly paid by Delia Cloutier P. Morey of Spencer in the County of Worcester

of Massachusetts, the receipt whereof I do hereby acknowledge, do give, grant, bargain, sell, convey and confirm, unto the said Grantee and her heirs and assigns forever, - a certain tract of land with the buildings thereon situated in the town of Warwick near Richmond, N.H. line and known as the Fenno Farm, containing forty-four acres more or less ...

Also the following personal property: one horse, three cows, one heifer, one swine, one sheep, two geese, farm wagon, one express wagon, one sled, two sleighs, one mowing machine, one horse rake, two plows, one harrow, one cultivator, small tools, horse hay fork, rake, iron bars,

chairs, sap pan, buckets, twenty eight hens, chickens, iron kettle, scythes and snaths, harness, cream separator, and whiffletrees, one churn, butter maker; all the wood cut on the farm and all of the potato bins in the cellar, ladders, being the personal property now on the place.

Possession to be given on or before May 27, 1910. ... To Have and to Hold the said granted, premises with all the privileges and appurtenances to the same belongings, to the said Grantee and her heirs and assigns, to their only proper use and benefit forever. ..."

Witness our hands and seals, this twenty first day of May Anno Domini one thousand nine hundred and ten."

Hard Times, 1924

—Notice published in the Enterprise
and Journal Newspaper, Orange, MA,
August 1, 1924

Mortgagee's Sale of Real Estate

By virtue of a power of sale contained in a certain mortgage deed given by Anna M. Whitney, of Brattleboro, Vermont, to Archie D. Jennings, of Winchester, State of New Hampshire, dated September 20, 1922, and recorded with Franklin County Deeds, book 654, page 262, for breach of the conditions named in said mortgage,

and for the purpose of foreclosing the same, will be sold at public auction at the Town Hall steps, in Warwick, in said county of Franklin on SATURDAY, AUGUST 9, 1924, at two o'clock in the afternoon, all and singular the premises conveyed by said mortgage deed, …

Said premises will be sold subject to the aforesaid mortgage to said Cheshire County Savings Bank and accrued interest thereon, and subject also to the taxes for 1924.

Everlings

Wonder how we can be
content beneath these posts
and beams, insulated from
the world outside.
Shed snake skins and rodent
skeletons fill the crevices
in lath and plaster walls

where the laughter of ladies
titters amongst the rooms
covered in faded pink roses
and soot. Outside the moon
fills with light, illuminating
the night where owls blink
and hoots are given back
to the lone coyote bark.

Prohibition, 1929

Night becomes a different country
when the regulars drive up the road.
Billie's black terrier starts to bark
at each rap of knuckles on the door.

Boots climb the narrow staircase,
rooms bloom with cabbage roses,
as the scents of sweat, moonshine,
and sweet perfume saturate the air.

From downstairs, come the sounds
of cards shuffling, the old Victrola
scratching out Louis Armstrong
and Al Jolson seventy-eights.

In one hundred years, our names
will be forgotten but this house
remains a witness to thirteen years
when the country meant to outlaw

sin but merely moved its purchase
to the outskirts of a righteous town.

Speakeasy, 1935

They come as darkness falls,
eager footsteps with furtive
glances up and down the road.
Whatever circumstances may
have drawn them to our door,
we welcome each one inside.

In this place, truth and lies
often wear the same disguise.
Secrets remain safe with us—
nothing they say here leaves
though later, we will whisper
whatever sorrows they share.

They toast with amber courage,
then follow us into dim rooms
where kerosene lamps flicker.
Some hold us a little too tight,
but most just want the comfort
of any woman's warm bosom.

When their breath gets heavy,
we listen for the mantle clock,
counting each half-hour chime.
They will rise again and leave
before morning's naked eye
shines down on us once more.

Once upon a time ...

When I was small, Papa gave me
a china doll in a blue silk dress.
I'd brush her blond hair each night
while Momma read me fairy tales.

Now I spend early evenings waiting
for a different bedtime and listen
to the stories men tell themselves
when they reach for me in the dark.

I watch them put on their other lives,
return to their wives and daughters.
But I wonder if they think of me
as they work in fields or factories.

Afternoons, I walk into the woods,
as birds compose their love songs.
I look for lady slippers and trillium,
a bit of beauty I can keep in a jar

that I'll place next to the headboard
on an old trunk from home—my hope
chest, where a doll with golden hair
waits, her glassy eyes shut tight.

The Renaming of Absence

You play your mournful music.
I know what you want—
      the moon and stars,
but I am fresh out of constellations.
Floating through this black space,
I can no longer take a breath,
a familiar heat pulls me down.
Loving you always burns me—
the want takes hold
before my senses can kick in,
leaving some part of me sore
for days, remembering and raw.
I hear the piano fingering desire
through the distance between us.
But I know these scars by heart.
I've heard this all before.
Now the clarinet howls, baying
at the moon's tired face.
Look up—count the stars,
      I am no longer there.

The Ruined House

With or without lust—
you shall not enter me again.

Beyond redemption, I am
a shell of splinters.
            Undone by desire.
Filled with danger.

My timbers can no longer
            hold emotion.
They lean beneath the weight
of sky, shattered into pieces.

Tonight, nearby
            in the mast of a maple,
one bird's steady singing.

A threnody of brokenness
inside each burst of longing.

George Rivers, 1883-1963

*Warwick News May 3, 1937: George F. Rivers of Richmond Road
was found guilty in Orange District Court of maintaining a house
of ill fame ....*

I've seldom known a trouble
that liquor couldn't solve.

Rumor was I won this farm
in a game of high-stakes poker

then began my bootleg business—
corn whiskey and bathtub gin.

The girls came later, proving
that every pleasure has its price.

Sunday mornings we all prayed
that God would forget our sins.

I was the only one He punished—
hard time in a cold prison cell.

Now Billie tends her flowers
and I wind the old Victrola

wishing for what came before
rheumatism and bankrupt dreams

until I'm buried deep in the back
of that same damn cemetery

with all those folks who believed
they were holier than me.

The Last Lady, 1930-1980
for Billie

There are stories told
about the lone woman
who inhabited this house
for fifty years. She kept herself
to herself, with no apologies.

Before indoor plumbing,
she owned a telephone
so the farmer down the road,
could call to warn her
when police headed her way.

She kept guinea fowl, loud
hens with polka-dot plumage
known for raising a ruckus,
sounding sirens of alarm
whenever they sensed danger.

Tough living and old habits
carved a long, stubborn streak.
Surviving the depression,
she fed guests pigs' ear soup
served up with stale bread.

But every spring, she cut
a floral bouquet for her sister,
deep purple irises arranged
in a slender antique vase
of gleaming carnival glass.

And at midnight, on the last
night of December, she'd walk
the 200 feet to New Hampshire,
place one foot in each state
and drink a toast to one more year.

-IV-

Soon after Billie's death, the farm became vacant, fell into disrepair, went through an abandoned restoration attempt, and was put on the market again in 1999. During that period, several sale transactions by prospective buyers failed. In the fall of 2000, my husband and I purchased the farmhouse with twenty-eight-acres of mostly wooded land.

Restorations

The Weeks descendants must have felt strong ties and a deep love for the farm: Caleb and Sarah's grandson, Caleb Mitchell, purchased the farm back in 1865, then sold it to his Aunt Angeline (Caleb and Sarah's youngest daughter) in 1870. However, the Civil War and influenza outbreaks contributed to difficult economic times, and the farm was finally sold out of the family in 1873.

The Long Way Back

I remember when you found me
        long ago, wandering
                through the forest.
I felt rescued by a knight; shining—
        our bodies seamless
as we tightened around each other.

But now you've left me
        in this strange place,
                where I've lost my way again.
How could I know the crumbs of attention
        I threw toward you
would be devoured by our young?

I'm stuck in this cottage
        covered by woods and longing
                for a new stove.
Perhaps I can burn my way out,
cut down and consume
        every tree that's grown in my path.

Tonight, though only an echo
        of moon hangs above us,
I will find you—
                I will lay my head on your chest,
and your heart will sound my way back

Home Restoration

... but the rooms are small and mean
and so papered over with secrets that
even their shape is uncertain ...
—John Ashbery, *The Ridiculous*
Translator's Hopes

They decide to find out
if passion has an expiration date
when their
empty nest threatens to
         untangle. Goblets—

delicate, decorated in dust, flower-
etched handmade in Rumania—
seem important for this occasion. Such
clarity might last throughout
         dinner repartee. Red
oak-casked, dubious bouquet. The pasta

is ruffled—she thinks Paesana means
friends, he knows of course it doesn't.
Strange marinara.
         No matter. Now that
her menopausal meltdown's passed,
spelunking perhaps? She suspects
it's too late. Split logs whisper
         from the grate
of the beehive oven. He pats
her head and considers
         whether or not
the esteemed revolutionary hero
who built their sturdy house

might just roll right out
      of his ancestral smallpoxed grave
to know what went on here
during prohibition. Rumor
was the "ladies"
avoided arrest by traveling
underground to the next state.
      Do cathouses have nine lives?

They climb nineteen steps to strip
      florid paper from the plaster and lath. If only
they could talk, amid a buzz of bluebottle-
fiddlehead flies gossiping.

Spring Forward

For months, the old horse
stood at the back gate,
staring into eternity.

This winter stole light
from my eyes—pried life
from my hands, too weak

to hold the breath
leaving the beings I love.
I have prayed with words

no one understands. Loss
is a language all its own.
Maybe prayers are the sap

that seeps from the maples,
sweet rivulets collected
in tin buckets with tented lids.

Or the crocuses I planted
last fall by the picket fence.
Even now, when I cannot

follow a straight line
of thought in my scrambled
mind, words still scatter

onto paper to wait for light.

Heaven

When you find yourself in a garden,
you are closer to your conception
of God, poking your fingers deep
in dirt. Weeds and worry have you
on your knees—praying for the birth
of each seed to take root and rise
through the soil to seek sunlight.

Mindful of each minor miracle makes
your eyes search the skies with hope
for enough rain to sustain each plant.
Suddenly, you succumb—a spectator
to growth gone wild, vines vying
for victory over all the empty earth.
Now you build your belief in bees
and butterflies, as pollination peaks
in the consummation of creation.

When the garden is spent, gratitude
gleaned for the food reaped before
frost finishes off the final harvest.
Light a bonfire in the midst of stones
that stand watch in a silent circle. Try
to summon seasons past and future.
Do not assume spring will come again
or if it does, that you will be present.
Plant your feet and feed the flames.

Catalpa

Who buried your one seed
to become this sturdy
trunk twisting toward sky?
For more than a century,
you stand tall in the center
of this hilly sheep pasture.

Ewes graze and lambs nurse
beneath your shady umbrella.
I pass under its gentle shadow
and feel your branches touch
then cool my impatient brow.

Lazarus of trees, still
barren in June. You are the last
to remember green, to grow
your robe of heart-shaped
leaves that sway and lift
in the slightest breeze.

Clusters of fragrant flowers,
then long brown pods dry
and drop their brittle casings.
Cigar tree, transplanted
from the land of tobacco.

What Lies Beneath

While rooting for slugs,
our Peking ducks unearthed
a small plastic statue planted
head down in the backyard.

The man who sold us this farm
seemed desperate to depart.
After papers passed he fled,
leaving most of his belongings
with no forwarding address.

When I found this odd
icon face down in the mud
and scrubbed him clean,
another mystery was revealed.

Superstition believes that
burying Saint Joseph brings
fortune to the sale of a house.
But if the saint is not found,
the home remains unsettled.

Now, Saint Joseph resides
upon a sunny windowsill
lined with colored bottles
and an old upturned horseshoe

where he has a wide view
of Shetland sheep in pasture
and every now and again
his gaze rests down upon
his three white-winged saviors.

Night Frame

While we inhabit our dreams, others
return to the world we leave behind.
The raccoon dons his mask, ambles
from the woods toward the henhouse
to test each latch. A tree toad squats
on the bottom stone step, surveying
his emerald kingdom. Fireflies
drift over the hayfield, emitting
their small sparks of desire. Slow
silhouettes thread the apple trees,
browsing on fallen fruit. Heart-shaped
signatures press into dewy grass.
Echoes of water lift from the pond
as peepers synchronize their sirens.
Suspended between deck rail
and porch column, moonlight silvers
the spokes of the orb weaver's web.
The spider at the center, waits
like God's steady eye.

Epiphany

the soul of the commonest object ...
seems to us radiant —James Joyce

Coffee poured into blue-speckled mugs,
birds perch outside the kitchen window,
the steady procession of black-capped
chickadees darting to the suet feeder,
while a queue of nuthatches and titmice
line up in the lilac's brown branches.

Then comes the red squirrel's antics,
cheeks chock full of sunflower seeds
as he tightropes across the porch rail.
Outwitting the young dog once again,
such bravado should be applauded
for its daily show of fearless finesse.

Notice the forgotten flag that salutes
the slightest breeze, its stripes forever
rippling colors of blood and freedom.
Today, think about all the women who
will walk out of doors to flee from war,
leaving their homes far behind them.

Sky Meadow

We search all our days
for a place called home,
hoping that walls and windows
will keep us safe inside.
As our skin grows loose
over our bones and our sight
softens the landscape,
we discover home might be
hidden in a meadow
amid murmurs of green
and sun-gold blossoms rising
all around our feet. This
will be the place we return to
when we remember our lives,
knowing the shelter that held us
as the water-blue sky came down
with a peace that could hardly last.

Darshan – Visions of the Divine

The word is the ultimate silence ....
From Suniai by Ajeet Kaur

near the pond's edge
the stillness of a frog sleeping
with one eye open

I remember now
gazing upon the lilies—
no mud, no lotus

moored to the bridge
a green boat rocks in silence
waiting to be free

bright blue dragonflies
compose cursive poems above
the pond's reflection

only one day each
orange daylilies trumpet
among the brown reeds

stones stacked upon stones
obey laws of gravity
as countries topple

a plain gray bird sings
his gift—this present moment
of pure melody

the curved stone path
ends where a small black figure
sits, hugging his knees

we live here, amidst
a world forgetting its purpose
lost in our pretense

bronze temple bells hang
no breeze visits the quiet porch
oh, to hear them ring!

-V-

Since moving here, I have come to understand that a place can possess its own power. Whether it was fate or happenstance that led me here, I have a deep affinity for this house and surrounding land. In 2018, I was half-heartedly opening some Christmas mail and was stunned to realize a card sent to us from a financial advisor I'd never met in California was in fact a photograph of our farmhouse. A photographer had taken the picture during a snowstorm around 2005, then sold it to a business greeting card company in Minnesota in 2012. The odds of someone unknowingly sending a card with this house on it are remarkable, but it is one of many mysterious events I have experienced living here.

The Healing of a House

Often, as I walk the perimeter of our farm with our dogs, I think about the Weeks family, those first settlers, and wonder about their lives and thoughts about the home they built here. They survived without electricity, running water, or modern medicine. They had no idea that their home would become a rural brothel during Prohibition nor the many changes and additions that their post and beam house would have over the 250 years of its existence. I also realize that the farm will encounter new owners someday and will shelter their families and dreams. In the end, we are merely caretakers of this house and land that we have come to love so much.

Gratitude

After an hour of down dog
and forward fold, we drive

the narrow road home, sun
sinking in a molten sky

where strips of clouds stretch
and wrap around the horizon.

You wonder about squirrels
digging acorns under road salt.

I wonder whether poetry
will ever come back to me.

After the barn chores, feeding
the crew of cats and dogs

I sit waiting, a zazen of hope,
legs crossed and mind open

watching each breath rise
then fall back into the world

which is dark now, but I hear
the muses, quiet, then question

their single syllable that calls
out into the still and cold night.

Pullet Surprise

The chickens are optimistic.
Each has an elegant name.

Gertrude and Sylvia
are Buff Crosses with exotic faces,
hard to tell apart.

Bernice, the Sex-link,
struts about the coop,
fluffing her emerald feathers.
She's the one the dog has her eye on.

Shy, yellow Letitia dashes
around in dizzy circles,
as if she has lost her head.

The Girls my husband calls them.
They run to him, perch on his arms,
peck at his wedding band.

Ruling the Roost

Rudy enters, comb erect, red-headed and ready,
side-stepping with his black-feathered feet,
tail plumage held high, gleaming like an oil slick.

The young pullets, all smitten, fall under his spell.
The hens, old libbers, resist his cocksure advances,
knowing a rooster's not needed to lay fresh eggs.

But Rudy's undaunted and patrols the perimeter,
his speckled chest puffed, fluffing his ruffled red collar.
He approaches each grand dame, with a majestic sweep

of one scarlet wing held out like a matador's cape.
Though the old hens appear unimpressed, one by one
he woos them away from their maidenly habits.

Now Rudy boasts all day, horny, henpecked, happy.

Gardening with Billie

Blue jays scream and fly over
scattered scratch feed, then land
in the apple tree to lob complaints

at hens huddled in a greedy circle.
I dig up the yellow irises to replant
them away from chickens' pecking.

Your peonies are gone, shadowed
by the towering honeysuckle bush,
where bees bumble in pink blossoms.

I tear out clumps of horsetail, an herb
known for helping ailing kidneys.
Spearmint spreads over the pasture.

We are joined by what we plant, hands
dug deep in this soil that grew crops
and cows for two hundred years.

Now to sow sustenance for the heart.
I poke marigolds and nasturtiums
around tomatoes and rows of beans.

When they bloom, I'll gather bunches
to fill your green carnival vase, then
we'll celebrate with a mug of mint tea.

Permission

Cool autumn wind parts the uncut meadow.
I call to the young dog who rushes ahead.
Untrained and unrestrained, he veers
down the deer corridor leading deep
into a dense stand of pines. I hear the distant
jingle of his tags and the sleigh bell tied
to his collar—warning bears and hunters
that he is not game.
                              Finally he returns,
then runs into high brush where he flushes
a flock of turkeys into a burst of flight
to roost high in the trees with loud squawks
and I think I can sense the old dog's presence—
feel again the snap of the chalk line
that draws two canine souls together.
The new pup honoring the old friend,
whose gift allows me to travel this path
once more.

Oh, to Be a Dog

Today is dark, thunder
and a steady downpour.

Outside the back door,
the chickens are wet,
and yet too stubborn
to return to their coop
where it is dim but dry.

The sheep have vanished,
no doubt crowded beneath
the horse standing inside
their weathered red barn.

The calico cat shuts her eyes
while steadily kneading
the soft blanket at the end
of the empty queen-size bed.

But both dogs are wagging
their tails beneath the hook
where their leashes dangle,

because dogs never fail
to embrace their beliefs
that beyond the front door
shines the brightest blue sky.

Winter Storm

In the first snow, we walk
down the unplowed road.
Both dogs, unleashed, run
in zigzags ahead, bear
bells jangling on collars.

After a mile or longer,
we reach the red slashes
that tell us to turn back
before time runs out
as dusk drifts down.

We listen for gunshots—
black powder discharge
that peppers the silence.
The deer have hidden deep
in stands of pine and fir.

The way home seems short.
But the final incline's climb
is tough on creaking knees.
The dogs have disappeared
over the rise to sit and wait

next to the dark green door.
Inside is a woodstove, hot
tea in glazed mugs, apple
cake, and the evening news
to bicker over until bed.

Yet when I lie counting
both sheep and blessings,
the familiar prayer I'll add
is to ask for one more day
just the same as this one.

The Keeping Room, 2020

I light the woodstove, then
lean against the cracked lintel,
watching the flames' shadows
rise in the quiet of this room.

I will never know the stories
of all the women who cooked
meal after meal for the last
two hundred and fifty years.

How they baked thousands
of loaves of bread in the beehive
oven, stirred stews in iron pots
hung from the swinging crane.

Sometimes, I imagine a room
full of fevers, nursing mothers,
chairs and cradles rocking,
and the flutter of bible pages.

If the hearth truly is the heart
of the home, this space retains
the echo of every person's soul
and the dreams they cherished.

What this room forever keeps
are the secrets of those who stood
right here, holding themselves
and all they loved close to the fire.

The House Speaks

Two centuries, I have stood
as the land changed around me.
Trees towered, disappeared
as forest became pasture
and then forest once more.

I remember strong men
who nailed posts and beams,
singing the hymns of beginning.
Clapboards dressed me then
and windows of single panes.

So many coats of paint, peeling,
scraped, then wooden shingles.
Green, then red, then green again.
Electric wires entered my walls;
iron pipes snaked into my cellar.

Most can no longer hear the voices
but I hear their echoes, the laughter,
the sorrows, and sometimes anger.
All the souls who have lived here
have left the imprint of their spirits.

As time settles my frame, timbers
creak a steady lullaby to summon
the ghosts each night who keep
watch in constant vigil to protect
and turn away any threat or harm.

All I ask is for you to never leave
me empty. Fill me with flowers
and music. Keep a lantern burning
in the window, a beacon of light
that will welcome you back home.

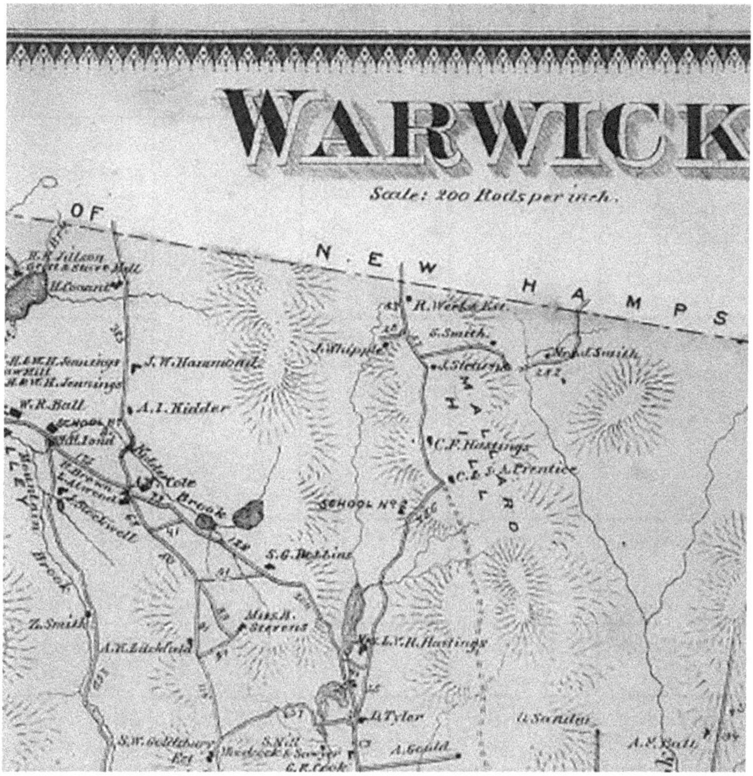
WARWICK
Scale: 200 Rods per inch.
OF
N E W H A M P S
J. W. Hammond
A. I. Kidder
W. R. Ball
C. F. Hastings
S. G. Robbins
Z. Smith
D. Tyler
A. Gould
Brook

Grantor	Grantee	Date	Book#/ Page#	Notes
William Weeks	Richard Weeks	approx. 1770		Built farmhouse on Samuel Weeks land grant
Richard Weeks JudithWeeks	Caleb Weeks	03/26/1801		will & testament Richard bequeathed-property to his son
Caleb Weeks Sarah Weeks	Richard Weeks	12/18/1855		will & testament Caleb bequeathed Property to his son
Caleb Weeks	William Weeks	01/18/1860	00222/432	$100 / 10 acres prop. on NH line
Richard Weeks	Elisha M. Davis	06/30/1863	00240/192	$840 / 63 acres
Elisha M. Davis	Caleb W. Mitchell	07/03/1865	00253/42	$673 /63 acres
Caleb W. Mitchell	Angeline Bishop	11/21/1870	00286/95	$600 /63 acres (Caleb Weeks' grandson)
Angeline Bishop	Melissa Bates	08/26/1873	00306/361	$1000 Sale 63 acres (Caleb Weeks' daughter)

Grantor	Grantee	Date	Book#/ Page#	Notes
Melissa Bates	Edward H. Fenno	11/28/1873	00310/108	$800 Sale now 44 acres
Melissa Bates	Edward H. Fenno William P. Coburn	10/21/1876	00327/248	$250 /20 acres (split off land)
Edward H. Fenno William P. Coburn	Catherine D. Hastings	08/22/1878	00338/231	$20 /20 wooded acres
Edward H. Fenno Sarah E. Fenno	Mary Ellen Whipple	04/06/1886	0406/1886	$850 Sale
Mary Ellen Whipple Eugene E. Whipple	Ann M. Hastings	05/31/1893	00430/379	$850. Sale
Ann M. Hastings	Alfred Swanson	09/18/1893	00432/235	$900 Sale
Alfred Swanson	Morey Delia Cloutier	05/31/1910	00563/43	$1250 Sale included extensive livestock & property
Morey Delia Cloutier	Anna M. Whitney	09/26/1922	00688/61	$900 Sale
Anna M. Whitney	Archie D. Jennings	08/18/1924	00690/353	Auctioned after default
Archie D. Jennings	Walter D. Sawyer	12/02/1924	00711/326	Gave half ownership
Archie D. Jennings Walter D. Sawyer	Arthur W. Farrington	12/09/1927	00739/246	Sold as Fourth Tract

Grantor	Grantee	Date	Book#/ Page#	Notes
Arthur W. Farrington Earl W. Moody, Adm. Wm. G. Moody, Est.	George F. Rivers	02/11/1935	00801/336	
George F. Rivers	Bernice Wisk	02/18/1941	00841/28	Ownership transfer during prison term
Bernice Wisk	George F. Rivers	10/04/1946	00883/362	Ownership transfer back after prison
George F. Rivers	Benjamin Delmolino	11/27/1948	00919/85	Foreclosure
Benjamin Delmolino	George F. Rivers	07/12/1951	00858/38	Transfer/Re-mortgage
Alfred Delmolino Jennie Delmolino etc.	Bernice Wisk	04/05/1954	01000/213	Transfer of deed after B.Delmolino death
Bernice Wisk	Helen Minkler	01/06/1986	01921/166	Sister added as Joint Ownership
Helen Minkler	James S. Lancia	01/20/1999	03451/127	$85,000 Sale
James S. Lancia	Timothy J. Millunzi	09/26/2000	03678/193	$145,000 Sale

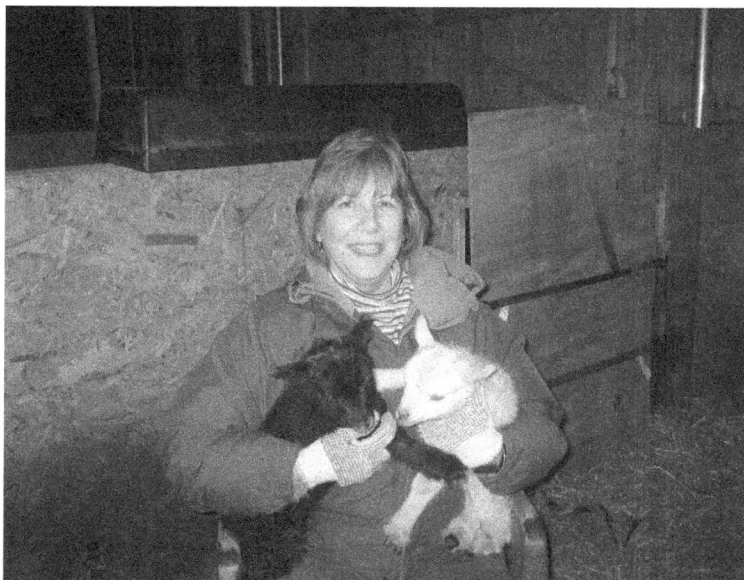

About the Author

bg Thurston lives with her husband on a sheep farm in Warwick, Massachusetts. After a career in computers and finance, she received her MFA in Poetry from Vermont College in 2002. She has taught poetry courses at Lasell Village, online for Vermont College, and conducts poetry workshops.

Her first book, Saving the Lamb, by Finishing Line Press was a Massachusetts Book Awards highly recommended reading choice. Her second book, Nightwalking, was released by Haleys in 2011. Her third book, The Many Lives of Cathouse Farm/Tales of a Rural Brothel, is the culmination of a decade of historical research about her 1770's farmhouse.